maths on display

Creative activities for the teaching of infant maths

$$1+2+3+4+5=15$$

by Barbara Hume and Kathie Barrs

contributing author Sandy Guertin
illustrations by Kathie Barrs

First published in 1988 by
Belair Publications Ltd.,
P.O. Box 12, Twickenham, England TW1 2QL
© Barbara Hume, Kathie Barrs and Sandy Guertin
Designed by Richard Souper
Photography by Kelvin Freeman
Typesetting by Tameside Filmsetting, Ltd.
Printed and Bound by Heanor Gate Printing Limited.

ISBN 0 947882 90 X

Acknowledgements

The Authors and Publishers would like to thank the children and staff of Orleans Infants School, Richmond-upon-Thames, for their co-operation in the making of this book.

They would also like to thank Darell Primary School, Richmond, for permission to include photos of their school calendar [P.61].

Contents

Introduction

- In presenting this book we wish to offer infant teachers practical ideas for producing stimulating and exciting displays of mathematical work.
- The activities are arranged under the headings of Number, Measuring, Capacity, Shape, Weight, Money and Time.
- Although to some extent the activities show the development of concepts, for example, from the use of non-standard units of measurement to standard units, it must be stressed that we do not aim to provide a syllabus or curriculum document.
- Within the chapter entitled Number, there are ideas for recording number bonds, for displaying number lines and for incorporating number work into popular class 'themes'. We would like to encourage you to take the recorded work out of exercise books and put it onto the wall, on the floor, or hang it from the ceiling!
- In subsequent chapters we suggest that, instead of trying to fit mathematics into your project work, that you consider making a maths topic your starting point.
- Within each chapter there are suggestions for ways in which a topic might be introduced, for things to collect for display, maths activities, art and craft ideas, together with further suggestions for extension across the curriculum.
- We feel that displays should not only reflect the work carried out in a class but should also stimulate and sustain the children's interest in a particular topic. Display tables can provide objects to handle, experiments to carry out, and materials to sort and classify. The children should be encouraged to take responsibility for making sure that the display area is kept tidy and attractively set out.
- We suggest you bear in mind the rich variety of multi-cultural experiences which may exist within your school and apply these to celebrations, activities, cooking, shopping, artwork, collections etc.
- While working with young children we have become aware of the close correlation between mathematics and art:
  - fitting a painting on to a piece of paper entails mathematical concepts, including balance and measurement.
  - drawing objects in relation to each other requires an understanding of ratio and proportion.
  - designing a pattern involves a sense of shape and geometry.
- Finally, the ideas that we suggest in this book are intended to make infant maths more enjoyable for you and the children.

Barbara Hume and Kathie Barrs
1988

NUMBER

Spring Maths

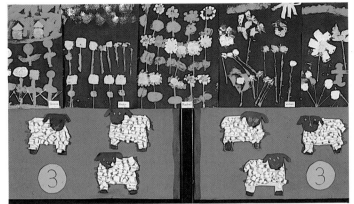

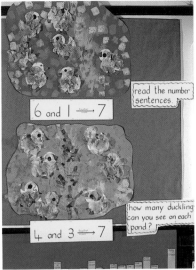

read the number sentences.

6 and 1 ——→ 7

how many duckling can you see on each pond ?

4 and 3 ——→ 7

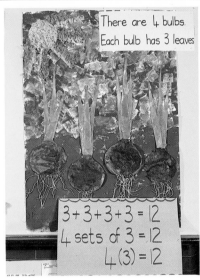

There are 4 bulbs. Each bulb has 3 leaves

3 + 3 + 3 + 3 = 12
4 sets of 3 = 12
4(3) = 12

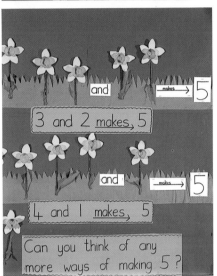

and ——makes——→ 5

3 and 2 makes 5

and ——makes——→ 5

4 and 1 makes 5

Can you think of any more ways of making 5 ?

Number bonds

- **Flowers in a vase**

  Make vases by stapling card shapes to the wall. Make flowers with tissue paper, straws, eggbox sections, crêpe paper. Children put flowers in vases and make the 'number sentence' with the prepared cards and a Breakthrough word-stand.

How many ways can you make 6 ?

| 3 | and | 3 | ——→ | 6 |

- Make a series of wall stories to illustrate number bonds. Where possible relate to a number rhyme, e.g.
  - i) ducklings on a pond – 'Five little ducks went swimming one day'
  - ii) tadpoles in a tank – 'Six porwigles' by J. Holder
  - iii) frogs on a log – 'Five little speckled frogs'
  - iv) swans and cygnets
  - v) lambs in a field
  - vi) eggs and chicks

5

Spring Maths
Egg maths

A dozen egg activities!

- Decorate large egg shapes with repeating patterns. Crayon heavily and put a fluorescent wash over the top for a really effective wax resist. (Some eggs with a straight line pattern, some with a curved line pattern).

- **Make egg number jigsaws**

- **Make decorated Easter egg baskets from a net. Add a handle.**

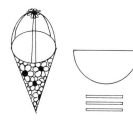

- Make Easter bonnets. Measure around head to make a headband. Decorate by sticking shapes on headband, e.g. chicken, egg, chick, chicken, egg, chick. Write on headband 'What comes first, the chicken or the egg?' OR make as a mobile around a hoop.

- **Eggbox maths.** Count in sets of six. Display eggboxes with unifix, beads, fircones, or decorated 'blown' eggs. To display on wall, paint recesses and leave empty.

6   12   18

Count in sets of 12   1 dozen – 12
                           2 dozen – 24
                           3 dozen – 36

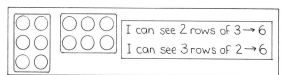

I can see 2 rows of 3 → 6
I can see 3 rows of 2 → 6

- Make a graph showing how children like their eggs cooked. Make the poached, fried, scrambled eggs etc. with various collage materials to stick on the graph.

- Cooking: Make fairy cakes by using the 'egg method' of balancing ingredients. Make a nest on top of each cake with butter icing and grated chocolate. Put sugar-coated eggs on the nests in 3's.

- **Matching 1:1 on a chart.**
  'Suddenly the egg cracked and out came.........

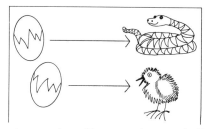

Match egg to picture with tape or streamer.
Write stories and display on egg shapes around the chart.

- Investigate egg sizes. How are they coded? Compare size and weight.
- Draw flow diagrams to show the life-cycle of creatures that lay eggs.
- Egg-rolling. Measure how far an egg can roll.
- Incubate eggs. Make a diary and record what happens.

Autumn Maths
Trees, fruit and seeds

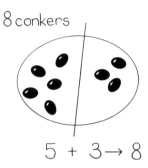

8 conkers

$5 + 3 \rightarrow 8$

- Ask children to collect acorns, cones and conkers. Take 'a handful' and scatter in prepared tin or dish (having taped or painted a partition line). Record the way the conkers have fallen.

Apples and pears

- Cut fruit in half and print to make sets on large apple-shaped or pear-shaped paper.
- Print apples and pears on tree shapes. Children make up their own number sentences.

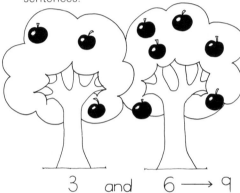

3 and 6 ⟶ 9

- Cut apples into halves, quarters, eighths. Dip into honey and give each child a piece to celebrate Rosh Hashanah (September).
- Count pips in apples. Plant them. Tell 'Johnny Appleseed' story (North American folktale).
- Weigh using apples, conkers, cones, acorns.
- Study symmetry of leaves: leaf printing, rubbing.
- Measure the circumference of trunks of trees close to your school.

Firework maths

'Remember, Remember the 5th of November, Gunpowder, Treason and Plot!'

Number bonds display:

Christmas Maths

- **'Days of Christmas'** display of triangular numbers

$$1+2+3+4+5 = 15$$

Other Christmas images can be used, e.g. 1 star, 2 bells, 3 angels, 4 snowmen, 5 crackers, 6 robins etc.

- Ideas for repeated addition worksheets, e.g.
    Draw 3 parcels in each stocking. How many altogether?
    Draw 5 baubles on each tree.
    Put 2 presents in each sack.

- Put wrapped presents of different shapes on and under a 'shape' Christmas tree.

- Make symmetrical tissue-paper window frames, e.g. snowman, angel, tree, candle (see Symmetry).

- Money: hold a Christmas market to collect money for charity. Calculate money spent, change, totals. (See page 52).

Advent calendar

- **Countdown to Christmas.** Put numbers 1–24 on the baubles of a Christmas tree. Investigate each number as it is opened. Display eight baubles on each of three trees. Hexagon, square or circle shapes open up into star shapes to reveal the pictures underneath.

8

Christmas Maths

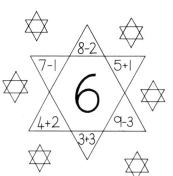

- **Make six-pointed stars** with art straws.
  Make two equilateral triangles and glue
  to backing paper as shown in photograph.
  Cut out and mount on foil. Write number
  bonds on points of star. Glue a silver 6
  in the middle. Display creative writing
  on star shapes – 'My Christmas wishes'.

- Cracker 'sums'. Colour the cracker according to the code. This can be
  adapted for any Christmas shape, e.g. bell, angel, candle.
  (As for butterfly sums, page 13).

- **Cracker dominoes** with two sections adding up to 10.

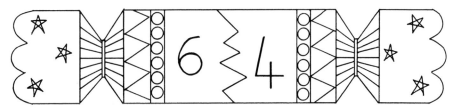

- Make a large Christmas tree shape by painting, printing or collage. Decorate
  with circular bauble shapes numbered 1–20. Link with tinsel according to
  different criteria, e.g. '+ 2', or 'join the odd numbers'. (See photo above).
  This idea can also be used for an individual worksheet.

- Make a wall story or class book:
  1 silly snowman skiing
  2 silly snowmen singing   } Make large sponge-printed snowmen
  3 silly snowmen skating

Number Lines

- **Make large numbers.** Children trace the numbers with felt-tipped pens to make rainbow numbers. Display as a number line.

  Match numerals to sets of shapes, or children, etc.

- **Whole school number line.**

  Each child draws a face on a round piece of paper. Group in 5's or 10's and pin to number line. Arrange on zig-zag string across the school hall.

- **Odds and Evens:** street of houses

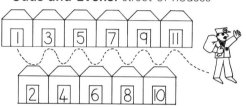

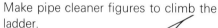

- **Make ladder** from corrugated cardboard. Make pipe cleaner figures to climb the ladder.

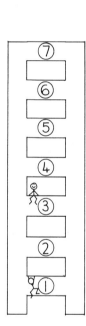

- **Number snake**

- **Children paint large teddy bears.**

  (Read *Teddybears 1–10* book, Susanna Gretz).

  Hang painted teddies on a washing line across the classroom, or pin on a display board.

10

Number Lines

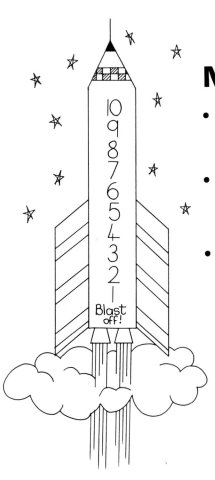

- **Countdown rocket**

- **Spiral snakes** made by each child in class. Circles are painted or crayonned, and cut.

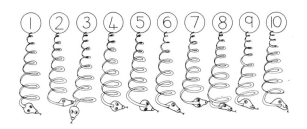

- **'10-in-a-bed'**
  Children paint faces on paper plates: patchwork quilt is made of individual squares, decorated by the children.

- **Hand cut-outs** (or prints) with number pattern 5, 10, 15, 20 etc. printed on palms to form a number line.

- **Chinese New Year:** Ordinal number line. Illustrate story of the animals racing. Paint characters: rat was 1st, ox was 2nd, tiger was 3rd, hare was 4th etc.
  Label with numerals and words: 1st and First; 2nd and Second.

- **Footprints** on floor, up wall and over ceiling. Draw around feet and cut out.

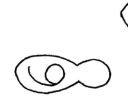

Machine Maths

Discussion: What is a machine? What does it do? What kind of machines are used at home? At work?

Collections: Ask children to bring in parts of machines, small machines, models, pictures and posters.

Space maths

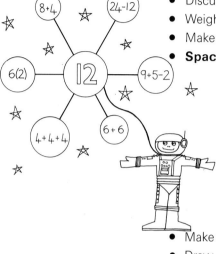

- Discuss large numbers: distances, number of stars, infinity.
- Weightlessness (See 'Cooking in a capsule', p.45)
- Make a rocket numberline. Count down from 20.
- **Space-station number bonds** (see photo p.45)

- Make a robot with, say, 20 or 30 Multilink cubes.
- Draw a robot on squared paper using 40 squares.

Machines at home

- Sort and classify machines used at home. Use a large picture of a cutaway house and either draw the machines or cut out magazines or catalogue pictures and sort them according to where they are used. Glue into the appropriate part of the house.
- Individual houses could be displayed together to make a street. Include machines used outside: vehicles, aeroplanes, cement-mixers, etc. to make a frieze.
- Sort out machines i) according to energy/power source
                        ii) according to use, e.g. for work or leisure.

Wheels

- Count in sets of 2 (bicycle) 3 (tricycle) 4 (car) etc.
- Draw large wheel shape. Divide circle into sections by folding, and paint each section with different patterns.
- Draw, paint and print cog wheels.
- Design futuristic vehicles.
- Make working machines and vehicles from junk materials or construction toys.
- Measure the circumference of a wheel: use a bicycle or trundle wheel.
- **Make an input-output machine** with a friend. Change numbers according to certain rules (e.g. add 2)

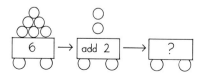

Can you guess the rule or process, given only the input and output?

Mini-beast Maths

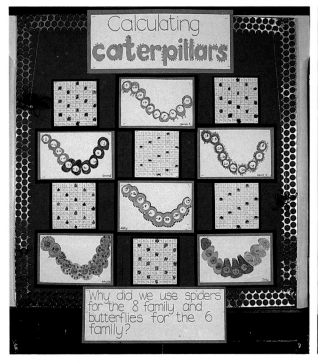

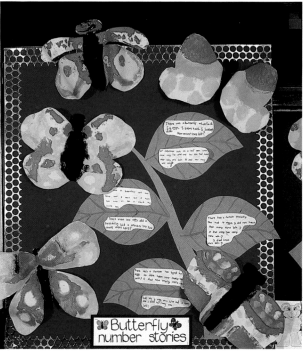

- Carry out a mini-beast count: how many creatures are found at different locations?
- Sort and group creatures according to attributes, e.g. the food that they eat and the places where they are found.
- Measure mini-beasts.
- Investigate: the number of legs, the shape of their homes, the symmetry of creatures, and their patterns and markings.
- Time: study life cycle of mini-beasts and relate to the changing seasons, e.g. through stories such as *'Charlotte's Web'*, E. B. White, Puffin.

Butterfly bonds

Colour codes, e.g.

5	black	8	red
10	purple	7	pink
9	yellow	6	blue

Ladybird: double numbers

i) papier mâché on a balloon, cut in half when dry, OR

ii) by building up a ladybird shape with screwed up paper glued on cardboard. Cover with layer of tissue paper, paint, and glue on the black spots.

Mini-beast Maths

Spiders

- Counting in sets of 8: Make spiders with pipe cleaners, black wool pom-poms or eggbox sections. Cut 'lacy' spiders' webs from crêpe paper.

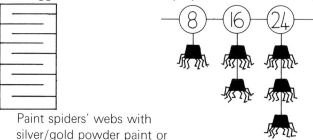

Paint spiders' webs with silver/gold powder paint or silver/gold crayons on black paper.

Make mobiles and hang as a number line.

- 100 square. Draw a spider in every eighth square, to count in 8's. (see photo on previous page).

Counting on a caterpillar

Use as worksheets (large format) or as a number line. Children invent number patterns e.g. Can you end up with the same number you started with?
OR Count in sets, 5, 10, 15 etc.

Bees

Explore hexagons: counting in 6's, making hexagons using six equilateral triangles, tessellations.

If a bee visits three flowers, what is the highest/lowest score that could be achieved? If the bee visits all the odd/even numbers, what is the total?

The flowers could be painted using water-based drawing inks, or collage, and glued on a printed and sponged background. (See front cover)

Snail

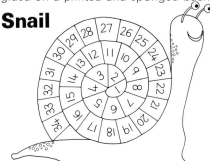

Use as a number line or board game.

MEASURING
Giants

poem: 'Giants' delight', Steven Kroll (see Book Ref. page 70)

Young children enjoy exploring the extremes of size. There is a wealth of 'friendly giant' stories, both traditional and new, which serve as a useful starting point for discussions about size. 'Jim and the Beanstalk' lends itself to the topic of measurement in particular, although many other giant stories can be developed in a similar way.

'Jim and the beanstalk'
(Raymond Briggs, see Book Ref. page 70)

- Jim needed to measure the giant's head for his wig. Measure around your head with a tape measure or strip of paper. Now compare with your friend's. Now measure your teacher's head. Is it much larger than yours? Why do you have to use a tape measure? Introduce the word circumference. Measure around other parts of your body, e.g. waist, chest, hips, wrist, ankle. Compare your measurements with a friend's.

- Jim's giant needed false teeth. How do dentists make precise measurements? Ask dentists for old moulds for display.
  How much food do you think a giant would eat for one meal? Make a giant's plateful of food with giant-sized hamburger, steak, giant-sized chips and peas.

- The Giant needed glasses. The print in his books was too small. What other instruments help us to see? Display microscope, magnifying glass and binoculars, together with a range of small objects to be studied through lenses (e.g. a shell, a feather, woven fabrics).
  *(Safety: Stress the importance of not looking directly at the sun – light and heat are intensified too, and can damage eyes.)
  Borrow books with large print from the library. Who might need these books?

15

Giants

- Make collage or paint picture of a giant.
  For Jim's giant: make large spectacles, wig and false teeth to fit the picture.
- Name your giant, and write adventure stories and plays about him/her.
- Make a collection of storybooks and poems about giants.
- **Collect 'giant' words,** e.g. huge, gigantic, big, towering, enormous, great, immense, vast, monstrous, massive, mountainous, colossal, mammoth, monumental, megalithic, mighty, stupendous, dinosaurian. Display words on a mountain shape, dinosaur, or mammoth.

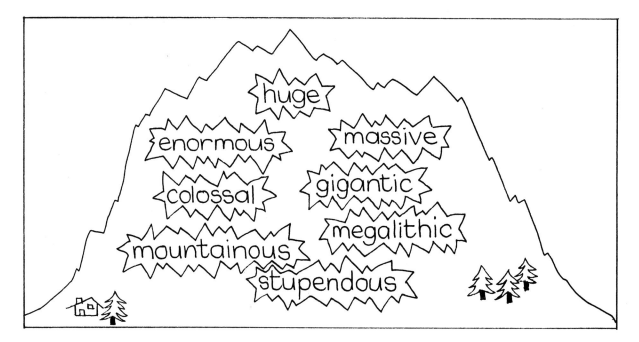

- Find out about Titan, Gargantua, Brobdingnagian, Gog and Magog, Cyclops, Goliath, Amazons.
- Study 'giant' creatures. Develop topic to include dinosaurs, large mammals.
  Refer to *The Guinness Book of Records* for largest, tallest, longest.
  Reproduce the shape and size of footprints of dinosaurs and living mammals. Compare with human footprints.
  Pace out length of dinosaurs in playground. Use metre ropes, sticks, trundle wheel.

Changes of Shape and Size

Changes in shape and size have long been a recurring theme in literature.
'FLAT STANLEY' IS FLATTENED!
(Read *Flat Stanley*, Jeff Brown – see Book Ref. page 70)

- Make individual 'Flat Stanley' pictures from shapes. Draw around logiblocks and cut out corrugated card. Decorate with paint, wool, sequins, buttons etc. **Label with 'flattened' writing**.

- Make large full-size 'Flat Stanleys' by drawing around children on corrugated cardboard. Cut out and dress, or decorate with materials. Make a class frieze of Stanley's adventures, rolling him up and being carried, being flown as a kite or as a picture in a frame.

- Write a story about what you would like to do if you were as flat as Stanley. Can you think of any disadvantages?

- Language of comparison: Flat Stanley was as flat as .... a pancake, a letter, a leaf, a postcard, a wafer biscuit. Collect flat things for display.

FLAT

'LENGTHY' THE DOG IS VERY L-O-N-G
(Read *'Lengthy'*, Syd Hoff – see Book Ref. page 70)

- **Make expanding figures** and display expanded on a wall frieze, or hang from a line.

Tail and legs fixed with butterfly pins. Head attached on a spring of card.

- Other figures: clown, Father Christmas, Jack-in-the-Box.

Changes of Shape and Size

- **More ways of making expanding figures:**

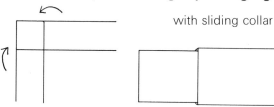

with sliding collar

by plaiting paper

by putting one paper towel
tube inside another.

- 'MRS. PEPPERPOT' KEPT shrinking!
  (refer *Mrs. Pepperpot* books, Alf Prøysen, Young Puffin)
- What could you do if you were suddenly very small? Write a story about your adventures – the advantages and disadvantages of being minute.
- Collect words and descriptive phrases. (Small, tiny, minute, little, miniscule, microscopic, infinitesimal, 'pocket-sized', 'fit on the head of a pin', 'knee high to a grasshopper'). Illustrate.
- Study very small creatures – mini-beasts. Make close observational drawings using inks, pencils or fine felt-tip pens for detailed work.
- Collect as many stories as you can about tiny characters and creatures.
- Collect and display models, for example trainsets, dolls' house, dolls, model cars, aeroplanes and trains, miniatures, 'ships in bottles'.
- Visit dolls' museum, toyshop, model museum or exhibition.
- Make miniature books. Collect old and new miniature books.
- Discuss: Why is miniaturisation sometimes necessary? (e.g. illustrations for postage stamps, micro-technology, making maps and plans, the use of Microfiche for storing information in a library.)
- Research: *The Guinness Book of Records* for smallest mammal, smallest bird, etc.

Ordering according to size

Discussion: Tell traditional stories, e.g. *The Three Bears, The Three Billy Goats Gruff*, using language of comparison: taller than, shorter than, larger, smaller, middle sized.
Compare heights of small group of children. Stand one child on a chair – discuss higher/lower.

Collections: Boxes of ribbons, lengths of braiding to be sorted according to length. Russian dolls, boxes within boxes, old nursery toy – 'nest' of trays. Collections of buttons, plates, squash bottles, packets, balls (i.e. things that come in different sizes).

Ordering according to size

Maths activities:
- Ask children to draw members of their families in order of height.
- **Individual worksheets** for earliest recording.

shorter than me	this is me	taller than me

shorter than a giraffe	a giraffe	taller than a giraffe

Lilliputian	Gulliver	Brobdingnagian

Other ideas
- Make a 'family of feet' chart. Children are asked to draw around the foot of each family member at home (include grandparents, friends, uncles, aunts). Cut out feet shapes and arrange on chart, ordering according to length. Label each foot with name (see photo p.21).
- On display table sort out objects, (e.g. Russian dolls), or make models according to criteria set by teacher. (e.g. 'make 3 bowls for the 3 bears').
- Make class books with illustrations on the theme "as tall as......" a tower, a giraffe, a giant, **or** "as long as......" a river, a snake. Make shape of book relevant to the topic.
- **Make expanding cards,** e.g. a snake → a longer snake, or a flower → a taller flower.

- Make illustrated wall stories, showing increase in size.

Growth

Babies

Discussion: Can you remember being small? What can you do now that you could not do then? What could you do then? (e.g. fit into small places.) Why do we talk about a baby's **length**?

Collections: Children bring in their old baby clothes, shoes, photographs, toys, hospital wristbands.

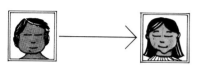

Activities:

- **Draw around first shoe and present shoe.** Cut out and mount on a chart. Make towers of Unifix cubes or Centicubes and compare lengths.

my shoe   my baby shoe

- **Display baby photographs in a set** and match 1:1 to present-day photographs of each child. Label.

- Draw pictures of baby animals and label in a set. Match to pictures of their parents, e.g. piglet/pig, calf/cow.

- Make own versions of *'Bad Babies Counting Book'* (see book reference).

Plants

- Look closely at seeds. Sort them according to size and draw them. (Collect a variety of seeds ranging in size from a coconut to the smallest flower seeds).

- Soak seeds and observe any changes in size.

- Make a growth diary or chart. Choose fast-growing seeds to sow, e.g. beans or cress.

  To measure:
  - i) Make close observational drawings (actual size).
  - ii) Attach a scale to the pot with a ruler or graduated strip.
  - iii) With very young children make towers of Unifix or Centicubes at regular intervals and display towers with the plant.
  - iv) Make graphs using graduated cm strip, or squared paper.
  - v) Dig up seedlings to measure root growth. Glue seedlings onto growth chart.

- **Make a wall-story or zig-zag book** to illustrate a 'growing' story.

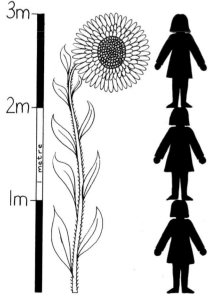

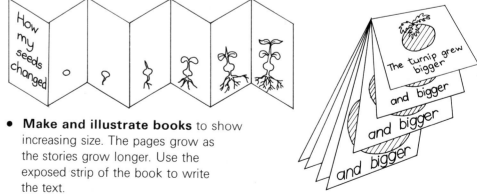

- **Make and illustrate books** to show increasing size. The pages grow as the stories grow longer. Use the exposed strip of the book to write the text.

- Grow real beanstalks as part of your 'Giant' display (near good light).

- **Cut large sunflowers at the end of the season.** Display in the classroom and measure, using standard or non-standard units of measurement.

From non-standard units to standard measures

Discussion: Why do we need to measure things?
Talk about distances, athletics, making things fit, buying material, clothes and furniture, building, height and span of bridges.
Vocabulary: height, width, length, span, circumference, cm , m , km.

Collections: Measuring instruments including tapes, rulers, gauges, calipers, cm cubes; labels from clothes showing cm ; height charts; plans and drawings showing specifications; dress pattern details.

Maths activities:

I. "About me" display

- Measure height. Display height measurements by
  i) using sticky paper strips, or graduated cm strips.
  ii) make a 'garden of flowers' as in photograph above.
  iii) draw around children, paint and cut out. Display silhouettes holding hands around hall or classroom.

- **Measure around head, waist, wrist, with strips of paper.** Glue on charts to compare, **or** use these measurements to make headbands, belts and bracelets.

  Thread beads onto shirring elastic,
  count number of beads on your bracelet
  and compare with your friend.

- **Measure reach**. Put large sheet of paper on the wall and record reach (both height and width) by using handprints. Each child uses a different colour paint.

This is how high I can reach.

This is how wide I can stretch.

From non-standard units to standard measures

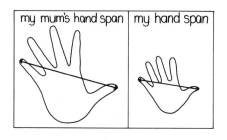

- **Measure handspans.**
- Measure the length of each finger, making five towers of Centicubes. Are they the same length?
- Measure (i) height when sitting (i.e. head to floor)
  (ii) from knee to floor
- Measure shadows at different times of the day.
- Measure length of hair. Draw sets of long-haired and short-haired children.
- Measure forearm with wool or ribbon. Glue onto a chart to display.

2. How far?

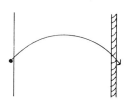

- **How far can you jump?** Cut a strip as long as the jump and glue on the floor.
- Measure stride lengths. Display as a 'floor chart'. Protect with clear adhesive film.
- How far can you throw a beanbag? a Wellington boot? a Frisbee? Use strides as an instant measure.
- How far can you make a paper aeroplane travel?
- How far can you make a Lego model car travel? Record distances measured in strides or metres and display with models.
- How far is it to the school office? (or toilet, hall, gate) Find the shortest route possible, with attention to safety. Draw a map.

3. Investigate

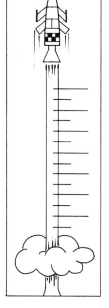

- How much ribbon do you need to tie a bow?
- Make a cover to fit a cushion.
- Make clothes to fit cardboard dolls.
- Measure the 'stretchiness' of a rubber band.
- Make a cube using a net. Now make a plasticine person or creature to fit inside your box. Make up a story about your creature.
- Design and make a label to fit a tin.
- **Design a height measuring chart for young children** (giraffe, sunflower, dinosaur, rocket, tower, clown on stilts). Use a graduated measuring strip, or make your own.
- **How many of your hands/feet fit along a metre stick?** Display with handprints or cut-out feet.

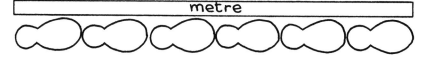

- Who can make the tallest tower using, for example, 10 paper cups, 20 bricks? Display and measure the towers.
- Draw sets of things – taller than a metre stick
  – shorter than a metre stick
  – about as long as a metre stick.

CAPACITY

Discussion: Which liquids do you have in your home? How are they packaged?

Collections: A good supply of varied containers – clear plastic ones are best. Plastic bottles, beakers, spoons, cartons, ladles, eggcups, funnels, balls (solid and airflow), liquid soap, Milton, commercial measures, sets of identical containers, e.g. clear plastic cups; sets of different containers which hold the same amount; tubing, syphon, sieve, water-wheel, flour-sifter, foil pie cases, moulds; labels for display 'holds more than' etc.

Maths activities:
- **Make a chart** providing vocabulary necessary for capacity work.

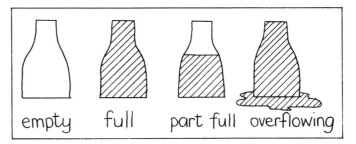

empty   full   part full   overflowing

- **Pour same amount of liquid into each of four containers.**
  Draw the water level in on a worksheet, or display containers on a table.

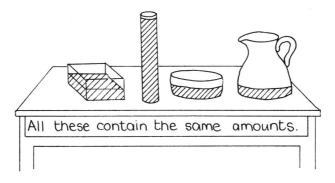

All these contain the same amounts.

- **Have a tea party in the home corner for the toys.** How many guests could have a full cup of tea from the teapot?

- **Make 'landscape' cards for the sand tray.**

Build a hill with a flat top using 6 cups of sand.

Next to it, build a hill with 3 cups of sand.

Make a river in between them.

Other children could estimate how much sand was used, and put flags in with their estimates written on. The builders would check for accuracy.

- Make pretend recipe cards for sand tray and playhouse use.
- **Diluting orange squash:** Allow the children to taste, smell and look at undiluted squash. Ask them to measure an equal amount into each of six beakers, e.g. two scoops.

Add water: 1st beaker – 2 scoops of water
2nd beaker – 4 scoops of water
3rd beaker – 6 scoops of water, and so on.

Discuss the results. Display on a window sill to see colour gradation.

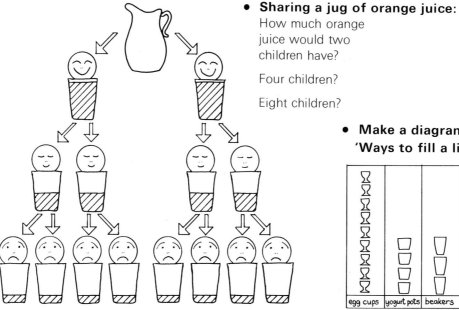

- **Sharing a jug of orange juice:**
How much orange juice would two children have?

Four children?

Eight children?

- **Make a diagram: 'Ways to fill a litre'**

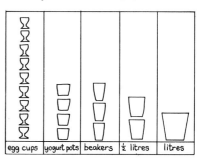

egg cups	yogurt pots	beakers	½ litres	litres

- Set up a liquid shop, using plastic containers and bottles filled with coloured liquids. They could be labelled with the amount they contain as smaller units of measurement are introduced.

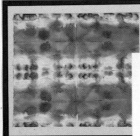

Art and Craft:

- Fold and dip:
  Fold a piece of kitchen roll several times. Dip into water and squeeze out between paper towels. Drop coloured inks or food colour onto the paper. Repeat on the back. Partly unfold to dry. Unfold and iron.
  (See photo above).

- Colour washes:
  Paint stripes of tempera colour onto wet paper. Use 'blown ink' technique for tree silhouettes. (See photo above).

- Marbling:
  Use either commercially produced inks or make your own using powder paint, oil and a few drops of white spirit.

- Still life of bottles:
  Use a selection of interestingly shaped and coloured bottles. Investigate reflections and shadows. Draw, using pastels or inks.

- Wax resist:
  Investigate – coloured crayon and black wash
              – black crayon and coloured wash
              – candle and wash

- Chalks:
  Investigate working on dry paper with wet chalks, and dry chalks on wet paper. Do they dry the same way?

- Tie dye using commercial and natural dyes.

- Batik

- Wash-out patterns:
  Draw a design on cartridge paper with faint pencil lines. Paint over these lines with white poster paint. Dry and gently brush Indian ink all over. Dry. Wash under running water. The poster paint will wash away leaving white areas and lines.

- Friezes:
  Underwater scene; pond life; cut-away house (showing water usage); how water is used in the community; **rainy day maths** (see illustration).

- Design swimming clothes, towels and swimming aids (lilos, rubber rings, etc.)

Language: **Word banks**

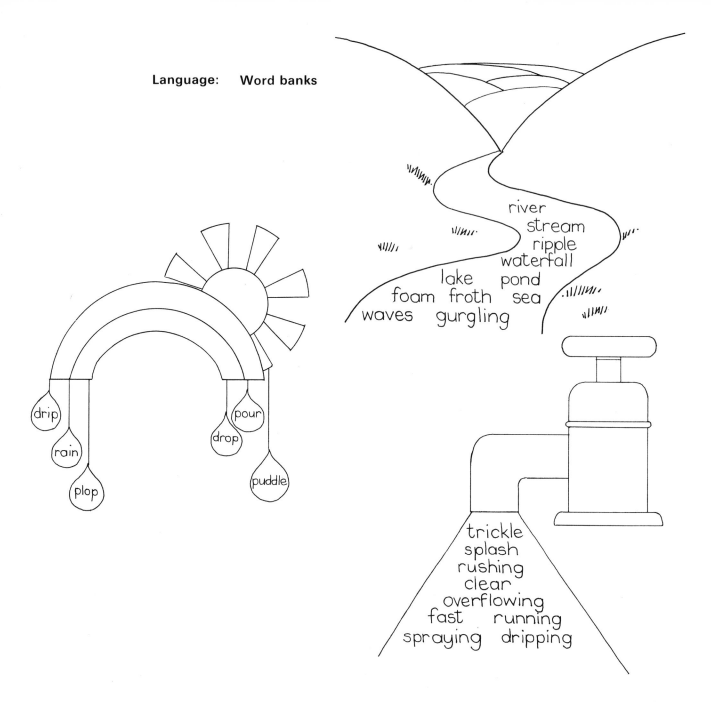

river
stream
ripple
waterfall
lake   pond
foam froth sea
waves gurgling

drip
rain
plop
pour
drop
puddle

trickle
splash
rushing
clear
overflowing
fast   running
spraying dripping

Stimuli for creative writing
- Study water – feel it, smell it, taste it, listen to it. Write or tape responses, and transcribe.
- Blow bubbles in the playground. Imagine you are trapped in a bubble. Where would you go? How would it feel?
- Write messages in bottles.
- Write about floods and storms.

Music, Movement and Drama:
- Mime, or dance to the following themes: shipwreck, storm, celebration rain dance.
- Make instrument or body sounds of water (e.g. fists tapping on chests, fingers drumming on floor)

Science: Investigate:
- Absorbency, washing, water in nature, solutions and mixtures, evaporation, freezing, displacement, floating and sinking.
- Make a crystal garden.

SHAPE

Solid Shapes

Discussion: Show children an object, e.g. a dice, a box, a tin of beans, a roller.
'What can you do with this shape?' 'Can it roll?' 'How many faces can you see?'
'What shape are the faces?' 'Could you stack these shapes?' 'What else can
you find that is this shape?' 'What could you make with this box?'

Introduce the names of solid shapes: cuboids, cubes, cylinders, spheres,
prisms, pyramids. Introduce vocabulary: faces, corners, edges.

Collections: Packets, boxes, tins, tubes, cubes, dice, chocolate boxes; labels from tins
and packets; balls, marbles and other things that roll (e.g. cylinders).

Maths activities:
- Sort boxes, tins, cartons and tubes according to different criteria, e.g.
number of faces; rolls/does not roll; faces with same shape/faces with
different shapes. Label sets and display.
- Cover each face of a box. Let children devise the best way of making a
pattern for each face. 'How many shapes have you drawn?'
- Paint each face a different colour. 'How many different colours have you
used?'

27

Solid Shapes

- **Draw a 'face' on each face of a box.** 'What shape are the faces?'
  'Are they all the same shape?' 'Are they all the same size?'

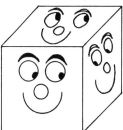

- **Take boxes apart and use the shapes to make nets for solid shapes.**
  Investigate making nets for cubes. Which combination of six squares
  (hexominoes) actually work?

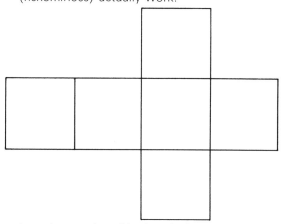

- Investigate cubes. Use interlocking unit cubes. (e.g. Multilink).
  - i) How many unit cubes are needed to make a 2×2×2 cube? A 3×3×3 cube?
    Display cubes and look at number pattern.
  - ii) How many different ways can you find of breaking a 2×2×2 cube in half?
  - iii) Build staircases and investigate number patterns.
- **Choose three different containers of the same type** (e.g. cylinders).
  Estimate which holds the most, and which holds the least.
  Find out by experimenting with sand, water or peas (pouring from one
  container to another). Display, showing relationships.

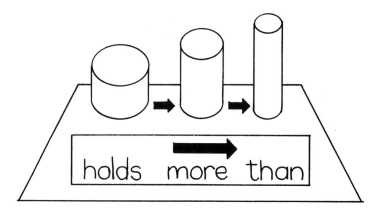

- Make skeleton shapes with plastic straw construction toys, cocktail sticks
  and plasticine, or art straws and pipe cleaners. Hang shapes as mobiles.
  White art straw shapes are effective as part of a 'black and white' display.

Solid Shapes

Can you see .....
a factory,
a camera, a face
and a machine?

Cylinder Landscapes

We painted the
insides of the
cylinders black.

Art and Craft:
- Make 3-D pictures by sticking boxes and tubes to a firm cardboard base. Make cylinder landscapes (as in photograph above). Paint insides/outsides in contrasting colours. Make machines or robot pictures with boxes painted with silver/gold paint or covered in foil.
- Make puppets with cylinders, cones, cubes and cuboids (cereal packets and tissue boxes).
  Write play scripts for the puppets. Make individual books, e.g. 'The Adventures of Mr. Silly Cylinder'.
- Print with the faces of 3-D shapes. Cylinders (both hollow and solid) provide an interesting number of effects
  i). Use ends of corks, cotton reels, tubes and straws.
  ii) Make rollers out of cotton reels covered in plasticine with patterns carved into it, or out of cardboard tubes with shapes or string glued on them.
  iii) Large or small painting/printing rollers. Apply paint to a printing roller with a brush. Paint the roller with different colours.

  Encourage children to create repeated patterns to cover the whole surface of the paper, and to overlap and rotate shapes.
- Display work on large cardboard boxes. Paint each face a different colour. Stack the boxes and glue or pin stories and pictures to the faces.

Solid Shapes

- Design a decorated gift box for a specific present, e.g. a bottle, a necklace, a kaleidoscope, a pair of slippers.

- **Make sophisticated junk models** or working, moving models. Make large group sculptures. Make a class playhouse, castle, train or spaceship out of large boxes. Make machines or robot pictures with boxes painted with silver or gold paint, or covered in foil.

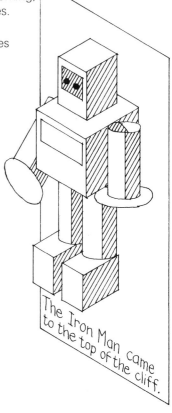

The Iron Man came to the top of the cliff.

- Draw solid shapes from different points of view.
- Still-life paintings: cylinders, balls, eggs, boxes.
- Consider why various things are packaged in particular containers (boxes, tins, bottles). Investigate shapes and materials.

Cooking:
- Cut and slice solid shapes. Cut slices of Swiss roll, 'tin loaf' of bread, Battenberg cake, etc. to illustrate prisms. What shape are the slices? Draw what you see.
- Peel an orange in different ways. Flatten the peel on paper and draw around it to investigate the surface area of a sphere.
- Make sausage rolls, 'silly cylinder' sandwiches, Swiss roll etc.
- Make food from other cultures, and experiment with shapes, e.g. Barfi (cubes), Vegetable Koftas (spheres), Spring Rolls (cylinders).
- Talk about shapes of utensils, packages and foods they are using: stock cubes, sugar cubes, cheese wedges, moulds and cutters, rolling pin, eggs, cherries.

Music: Collect musical instruments. Look carefully at their shape (cylindrical drums, spherical beaters, pipes).

P.E., Music and Movement:
- Small apparatus: roll balls.
- Gymnastics: somersault and roll sideways (stretched out or curled).
- Movement: Draw cube around your body.

Games:
- Guess the solid shape in a 'feely' bag.
- Guess a solid shape from its shadow.
- Guess a shape from a description of its attributes.

Squares

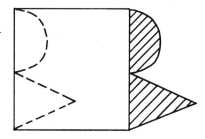

Discussion: What can you do with a square?
How would you describe a square to
somebody who had never seen one?
How is a square different to an
oblong, a circle, or a triangle?
Find squares in the environment (e.g. tiles, climbing frames).

Collections: Ask children to bring in things from home: board games such as chess, draughts,
snakes and ladders.
Checked material, tartans, ginghams, patchwork quilts, blankets of knitted
squares.
Artefacts with square faces: dice, boxes, stock cubes, sugar cubes, Rubik
cubes, tiles.
Unifix, Centicubes, Multilink materials, pegboards and 100 squares.
Cover display board in a checkered pattern of squares of contrasting colours.
Mount all work on square-shaped paper.

Maths activities: • **Investigate tessellations.** Use the
square as a base for tessellating shapes.
Cut from one side and add to the
opposite side.

Squares

- **Investigate the number patterns of increasing squares.** Use squared paper or square tiles. Display Unifix boards and Multilink apparatus.

- **Make squares larger** by adding another layer all the way around.

  How many have you added?
  Add another layer.
  Can you see a number pattern?

  Investigate the number of unit squares on the edges.

- **Investigate pentominoes:** patterns made with five squares touching along their sides.

  How many patterns can you make? Draw and cut them out. Make tessellations with the shapes.

- **Make pictures of square frames with art straws.** How many straws do you need? What is special about the length of the straws? What is special about the corners?

  Mount on square paper.

- **Halve-a-square.** Take a square of coloured paper and glue it onto square-shaped backing paper. Take an identical square, fold and cut it in half. Glue one half onto the picture, fold and cut in half the remaining half, and so on. Repeat this until the paper is too small to handle. Can you see a pattern?

Squares

Art and Craft: ● **Make a square mobile.**
Fold a square of thin card into quarters.

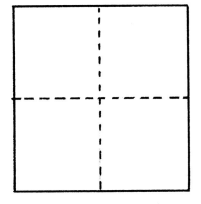

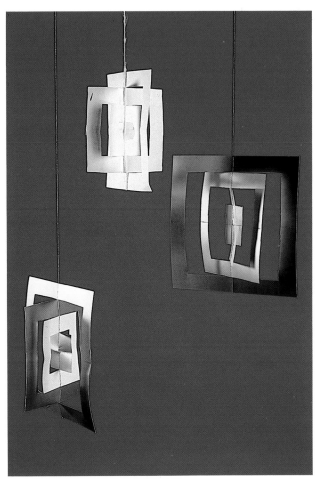

Hold the middle of the square and cut as shown in the diagram. Open out square. Glue string, wool or thread along the cut middle line of the square. Allow to dry. Now cut the dotted lines, and the square frames will rotate on the string.

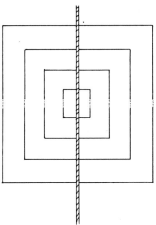

Use foil for Christmas decorations, or paint with gold or silver paints.

● **Explode-a-square:** Take a square of coloured paper and glue it onto square backing paper. Now take an identical square and cut it into small pieces. Arrange the small irregular shapes around the whole square to make a pattern or picture, making sure that all the pieces are included.

● **Sew a square:** Use rug canvas. Weave ribbons and thick wools around edge. Make a pattern of decreasing squares. Glue onto a square of felt. Make the square into a picture.

● **Mosaic patterns:** Cut very small squares from pages of magazine pictures. Sort out the squares into shades of colour before starting your picture. (Collect pictures of Roman/Greek mosaics — display with your mosaics).

Squares

- **Stretch-a-square.** Take a square of sticky paper. Cut strips across (making wavy or zig-zag patterns). Glue to backing paper, leaving gaps between strips. What shape have you made?

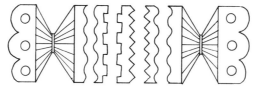

Patterns can be rolled and hung as cylinders, or made into the body of a cracker with tissue, crêpe paper, or foil ends.

- **Pattern-making on square paper.**
  Use decorated squares to make a patchwork design. Hang them back to back as a mobile, or make squares into a picture.

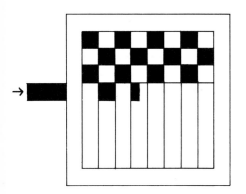

Use as part of a "black and white" display.

- **Weave a square.** Cut straight parallel lines on square paper or thin card. Weave different coloured strips through, under and over.
- **Print a square.** Use as many objects with square faces as you can find to print with. Try both ends of a Unifix cube, beads, Lego, bricks. Experiment with overlapping squares. Look at the shape of the overlap.
- **Design a square tile.** Make with clay. Print into surface and paint or glaze.
- **Design a patchwork quilt.**
- **Square rubbings and masking.** Cut out cardboard squares of different sizes.
  i) Arrange the squares into a pattern. Place thin paper on top and rub with crayon.
  ii) Arrange the squares on painting paper. Sponge over the top. Keep moving the squares to make a pattern.
- **Write your initials or your name with squares on squared paper.**

Language: Discuss sayings: 'back to square one', 'like a square peg in a round hole', 'a square deal'.

Circles

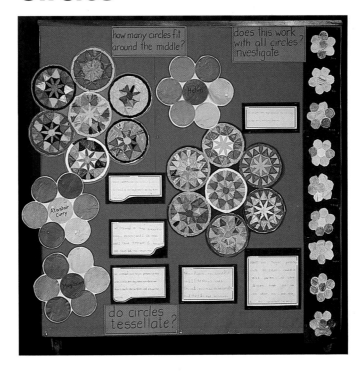

Discussion: What is special about a circle? How many sides does it have? How many corners? Find circles in the environment.

Collections: Coins, discs, medals, buttons, sequins, counters, wheels, hoops, bangles, rings, quoits, dials, plates, records. Solid shapes with circular faces: tubes, cylindrical boxes, cotton reels, cones. Materials, fabrics, wallpaper, wrapping paper with spotty, dotty patterns.

Maths activities:
- **Touching circles.** Use coins or counters to find out how many circles fit around a circle of the same size, with no overlapping. Does this work with all circles? (See photograph above for display idea using Rangoli patterns).

- **Make patterns using touching circles** and the spaces in between them. Do circles tessellate? Can you find some hidden creatures?

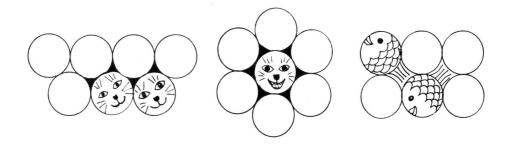

- Investigate overlapping circles. Print with ends of cylinders and tubes. Look at the shapes of your overlaps. Make patterns and pictures with over-lapping circles.
- How can you measure the circumference of a circle? Measure around a bicycle wheel or a trundle wheel.
- Investigate ways of drawing circles (e.g. using string, a compass, or circular objects).
- Fold circles of paper in half, quarters and eighths. Colour the segments.

Circles

- **Count on around a circle.** Investigate circles with 5 points. Count on in 1, 2, 3, 4's. Investigate circles with 12 points. Count on in 1, 2, 3, 4, 5, 7's. On a 72 point circle count on 19 or 20, or doubling every number (e.g. 1, 2, 4, 8, 16 etc.)

  Investigate the size of 'jump' needed to draw a square, an equilateral triangle, a straight line and a hexagon.
  Computer program "Circles"—SMILE.

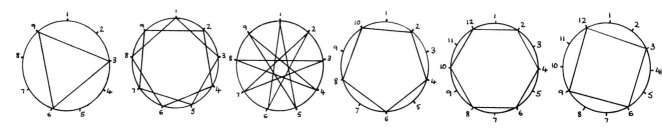

- **Stretch a circle.**
  Cut a circle into strips across.
  Glue the strips parallel to each other onto contrasting paper, leaving spaces between each strip. Can you see a different shape? (ellipse)

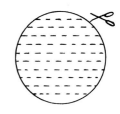

- Print. Make a straight, downward cut through a carrot or cucumber, and print. Now make a slanting cut and print. Compare the two prints. How are they different?

Art and Craft:

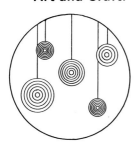

- **Explore a circle with paint.** Paint concentric circles carefully. Mix different shades of the same colour. Make the circles lighter going into the centre. Then paint a circle with the colour darkening as they decrease in size. Now compare the effect of the two circles. (Could be hung as a mobile).

- Give children two circles of white paper. Decorate with felt-tip pens (limit to two colours) making spirals, segments and concentric circles. Glue decorated circles onto a circle of material and use a variety of collage materials (sequins, felt, buttons, beads) to make pictures of animals, vehicles, people and flowers.

- Paint and decorate both sides of a large circle and cut out spiral to make snakes'. Hang as mobiles. (See line drawing p. 11).

- **Make a spiral picture with string or coloured wools on a glued circle.** Start at the outside of the circle, and limit the colours. This can be good practice for anti-clockwise hand-control.

- **Make a circle mobile.** Cut out discs or use milk bottle tops. Glue two contrasting colours together with the string or thread already sandwiched between them.
  Make patterns by repeating colours and sizes. Hang on hoops.

- Make bubble prints. Mix a little washing-up liquid with powder paints in round containers. Blow through a straw to make a cap of bubbles on top of the container. Lay a piece of paper on the paint pot. Overlap prints of contrasting colours. Print backing paper for mounting work for circle display.

Circles

- **Make streamers.**

  Staple several (8+) tissue paper circles together with one staple in the middle. Draw a spiral with a felt-tip pen. Hold at the staple and cut carefully along the line. Shake out the streamer.

  Experiment with different colours of tissue. How could you make a long straggly streamer? A shorter fuller streamer? Use your streamer in any of the following ways:

  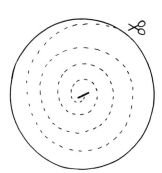

  i) Glue or staple onto rolled paper or cardboard cylinders.

  ii) Use as 'hair' for puppets.

  iii) Decorate a cone hat.

  iv) Decorate presents (see photo above).

- **Cone mobile.**

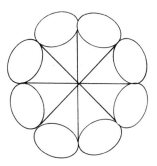

Make cones with segments of circles. Glue them together and hang as a mobile.

- Make a large, painted frieze of a circus incorporating as many circles as possible, e.g. circus ring, faces of audience, clowns juggling rings, seals balancing balls, dogs jumping through hoops, unicycle riding, etc.

- Design a picture plate.

- Tell the story of the Willow Pattern plate. Children make blue and white illustrations on paper plate or circle of paper with blue felt-tip pens or inks (see photo page 69).

- Print with tops, lids, tubes. Use pastry cutters to cut circles into polystyrene tiles. Use as a printing block.

- **Make a circle mobile.** See instructions for 'square mobile' (page 33). Hang circle mobiles from hoops.

Circles

- Look at newspaper pictures under microscope. Make dot pictures using the end of a straw to print. Draw outlines with pencil, or place thick felt-tip outline underneath as a guide. Use different colours, or different shades of the same colour.
- Make circular patterns on material with tie-and-dye techniques.
- Make pom-poms with wool. Add feathers, eyes, pipe-cleaner legs to make exotic creatures.

Language:
- Illustrate 'circular' stories such as *"No, No"* (Storychest, Level 1). Hang from hoop.
  OR
- **Stories involving life cycles of frog,** butterfly or hen (chick-hen-egg), seasons of year. Display on a wheel, fixed with butterfly pin, so that it rotates.

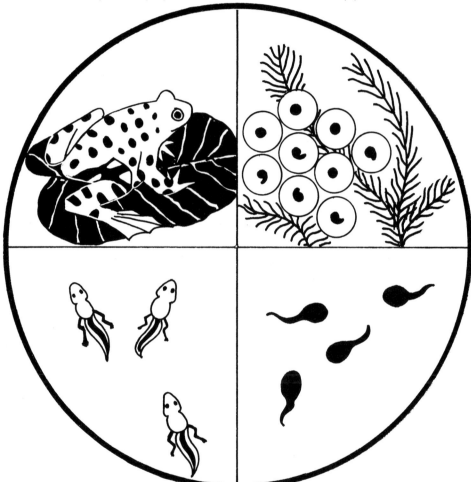

Cooking:
- Make round biscuits. Decorate as faces.
- Make a round cake or tart and discuss how to divide it into equal pieces.

P.E.:
- Ball games with children in a circle.
- Hoops, quoits.

Music and Movement:
- Children moving in a circle.
- Swinging movements.
- Turning on the spot – changing height for spirals.

Music:
Singing games in a circle: "The Farmer's in the Den"
"The Dusty Bluebells"

Triangles

Discussion: Find triangles in the environment, e.g. gates, paths, roof shapes, bridges, cranes, road signs.

Maths activities:

- Make triangles with geo-strips. Is it possible to make a triangle with any three of the strips? Why not? Make a triangle with three strips of the same length. What is this called?

- Folding paper to make triangles. Fold a square:
  - i) once to make two equal triangles
  - ii) twice to make four equal triangles
  - iii) three times to make eight equal triangles

  Investigate the number pattern. Open the paper and colour the triangles to display.

- Make triangles on nailboards with rubber bands. Transfer the designs onto dotted paper to display.

- Make "hexiamonds" from six equilateral triangles. How many different ones can you find? Do they tessellate?

- Investigate triangular numbers. Make patterns on pegboards, or Multilink pattern boards, and display.

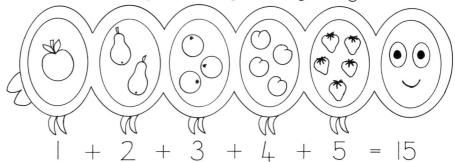

$$1 + 2 = 3$$
$$1 + 2 + 3 = 6$$
$$1 + 2 + 3 + 4 = 10$$
$$1 + 2 + 3 + 4 + 5 = 15$$

- **Make a wall picture** of *"The Very Hungry Caterpillar"* (Monday to Friday).

Monday Tuesday Wednesday Thursday Friday

$$1 + 2 + 3 + 4 + 5 = 15$$

- Make up your own triangular number story.
- **Draw concentric triangles.**
- Polysymmetrical triangles: rotate cut-out equilateral triangles to make designs.
- Cut up triangles and reassemble the pieces to make different shapes.
- Collect, make and display solid shapes with triangular faces, e.g. pyramids, triangular prisms, tetrahedra.
- Print with triangles: overlapping or tessellating. Use triangular sponges to print flower petals, leaves, daffodils.
- Design and make kites.
- Thread cardboard triangles and hang as a mobile. (Use needle and thread – no need to tie knots for each triangle.)
- Design safety warning triangles. Think of some imaginative symbols for use at home, in school, in the kitchen, garden or playground.

Cooking: Make toasted triangular sandwiches, samosas, pasties, turnovers and biscuits.

Language: Look at 'tri' words, e.g. tricycle, tripod, triplets, trillion, trilogy, tri-plane, triceratops. Write the words on triangles and display with a picture on the reverse. Hang as a mobile.

Oblongs

Discussion: Talk about oblongs in the environment, e.g. books, windows, doors, table-tops.

Activities:
- **Cut an oblong across the diagonal.** What have you made?

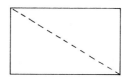

- Fold an oblong into a fan. Fix in the middle and open out to make a circle, or fix at the end to make a semi-circle. Use tissue paper or foil to make birds' or angels' wings.

- **Join a long thin band of paper and cut in half to make two rings.**

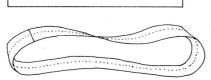

  Take another strip and twist before joining. This is called a Möbius band. Now cut along the length of the band. What happens? Experiment with bands with two or more twists.

- Take two identical oblongs of card and make two cylinders
    - one long and thin
    - one short and fat

  Do the two cylinders hold the same amount of sand? Find out by pouring.

- Investigate cuboids. Why are cuboids so often used for packaging?

- Find out about 'log-cabin' patchwork designs.

Bricks

- Look for brick patterns at school and at home.
- Take rubbings.
- Make brick patterns with Lego.
- Find out about: stretcher bond, header-bond, English bond, herringbone, Flemish bond, basket weave.
- Design a brick wall or path, using different coloured bricks and tessellations.
- Make brick patterns in clay or plasticine by pressing a face of a cuboid into it.
- Print a wall.
- Make a 'friendship wall'. Each child designs a brick with his/her name on it.
- Design and paint a mural.
- **Make an 'addition' wall.**

		36		
	16		20	
	8	8	12	
5	3		5	7
3	2	1	4	3

- Design a poster, a postcard, a postage stamp, a book-jacket, a stained-glass window, a rug.
- Make a paper sculpture picture using strips of coloured paper.

Symmetry

The Hedgehog Mirror, Eva Marder,
(See Book Ref. p. 70)

Art and craft activities provide an obvious starting point for investigations into the topic of symmetry, as very young children already show an awareness of symmetry or balance in their pictures. The techniques themselves are very enjoyable. Children love the surprise element of opening out cut-outs and 'blob' prints, and the very act of folding the paper produces an obvious axis of symmetry. The patterns and pictures of symmetry offer endless display possibilities.

- Use computer program "Islamic Patterns", Junior Maths, ITV, to print symmetrical patterns. (See photo above – cards on display table).

Art and Craft:
- Write name in black powder paint (use thick paint mixed with PVA glue). Fold paper to get print before paint dries. Trace over printed outline if needed. Lower-case letters stood on end can be made into 'space creatures' or 'faces'. Try white paint on black paper as shown in the photo above.

Symmetry

- Write words in capital letters, e.g. SYMMETRY, with mirror image below, to label display. Paint or crayon in the spaces. This effect can be applied to any topic area, e.g. WELCOME SPRING, MERRY CHRISTMAS etc.

  After some experience with paint and folding, older children will be able to mirror-write with felt-tip pens. Have mirrors available.

- Make 'ink-devil' patterns. Blob runny paint or ink on one side of folded paper. Re-fold and press carefully. Repeat using contrasting colours.

- Paint half a picture: half an apple, tree or an insect, and fold to make the whole picture.

- **String prints:**
  a) Fold piece of paper. Place a painted piece of string in the middle of the paper. Fold paper again, and keeping one hand firmly on top of the paper, pull one end of the string.

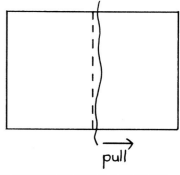

  b) Fold paper. Paint string and place on paper looped. Refold paper. Press with one hand and pull both ends of string with the other.

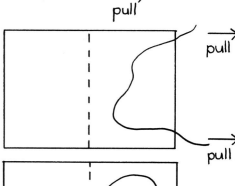

  c) Drop painted string onto paper in a pattern and press. Open paper and lift string.

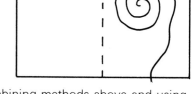

  Make pictures and patterns by combining methods above and using contrasting colours.

  N.B. As with all printing techniques, allow children plenty of opportunity for experimenting: have lots of scrap paper available so that they can try out different effects.

- Cut half a face or figure from a magazine. Glue onto a piece of white paper. Complete the picture by drawing the other half. (Make sure mirrors are available.)

- Tissue paper window frames.

  Fold strong paper, draw and then cut a shape from the folded edge. Paste tissue paper on reverse and glue on classroom windows. This activity has many applications at Christmas. Shapes such as tree, bell, angel, snowman, candle, are all symmetrical. The cut-out shapes can be decorated with tissue, sequins, glitter etc. and hung as a mobile.

  (Let children experiment with newspaper or kitchen paper. Individual children may want to make their own templates for a repeating pattern.)

Symmetry

- 'Reflective' paintings. If possible, arrange trip for children to observe reflections in water. Show photographs of reflections (a favourite topic with photographers).
  Use folding technique to paint outline of river scene and its reflections: Mix thick black powder paint with P.V.A. glue. Paint outline of picture with black paint on top half of folded painting paper. Fold to achieve 'reflection' and allow to dry. Now complete the picture with colour to cover the paper. (See photo above).

- On pegboards, Centicube boards, squared paper, make patterns either side of the axis of symmetry. Children can work in pairs, one child placing a peg with her partner copying movements. Display on table, with apparatus available for children to experiment.

- **Make 3-D shapes** by cutting a symmetrical shape on fold, and weaving (like a Chinese lantern). Ask children to fold card (A4 size) in half lengthways. Draw 'half shape', e.g. fish, on the fold and cut out. Make cuts at right angles to the fold, approximately 1 cm apart.

  Make a series of cuts along the fold – being careful not to cut the fish in half! Open out fish shape. Weave wedge shaped piece of card (tapered at ends), in and out of 'ribs' of fish. Twist wedge to make ribs stand out. This idea can be adapted for various symmetrical shapes, e.g. Christmas tree. Hang as mobiles.

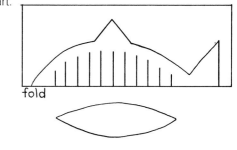

Symmetry

- **Symmetrical cut-outs.** Take a black sheet of paper and a piece of white paper half its size. Cut out half a symmetrical shape from the edge of the white paper. Glue white paper on the black. Place white cut-out shape so as to complete the picture (as shown).
This can be repeated.

- Children can paint or draw self-portraits by looking at themselves in a mirror. Glue onto a book, shaped like a hand mirror, or glue onto silver foil for display. (See photo on page 41.)
- Large cut-out figures of children can be made, showing them making symmetrical shapes with their bodies. (Draw around actual figures).

Science Activities:
- Experiment with kaleidoscopes; two hinged mirrors; concave and convex mirrors.
- Look at reflections on both sides of a shiny spoon. Children observe and draw images on spoon-shaped outlines (as in photo on page 41).
- Look at reflections in a shiny kettle and draw with silver crayons.

Language:
- Tell relevant stories, e.g. *Snow White*, and mount children's versions on foil.
- Children design pages for their own magic mirror book (See Book reference, p. 70).

Music and Movement: 'Mirror' dancing: one child moves, and a partner mirrors the actions.

P.E.: Make symmetrical shapes on apparatus, and on the floor.

WEIGHT

Discussion: Talk about weight and mass by discussing weightlessness in space and the effects of gravity.

What is heavy? What is light? When and where have you seen things being weighed? Why?

Have you ever been weighed? Can you think of things heavier/lighter than you?

Collections: Ask children to bring something heavy to school (with help of parents). Bring something light to school.

Collect different kinds of scales, balances and weights. Collect packages and labels with weights written on them.

Display all these objects on low tables so that the children can handle them and do experiments.

Meg on the Moon, Jan Pienkowski
(See Book Ref. p. 70)

Activities:
- Paint pictures of things being weighed, e.g. in a greengrocer's or supermarket, at the post office, at the baggage check at an airport, at a baby clinic, in the kitchen.
- **Make a large illustrated chart.** Draw pictures or cut from magazines.

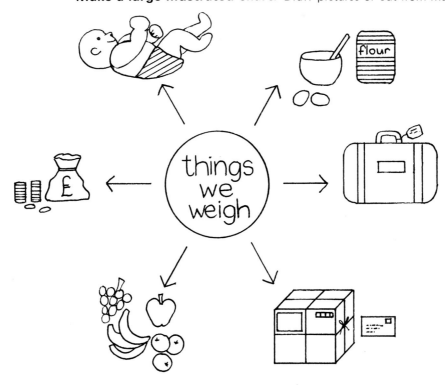

45

- Paint or collect pictures of a set of heavy things, and a set of light things.
- Paint real-life situations where heavy loads are being lifted or pulled
    - i) on a building site – cranes, diggers.
    - ii) fork-lift trucks and cranes on the dockside.
    - iii) weight-lifting.
    - iv) elephants working.
- Make a 'space' frieze showing the effects of weightlessness, e.g. 'Cooking in a Capsule' from *Meg and Mog* story. (See photo on previous page)

Comparing weights

- Make a large chart of obviously heavier and lighter things.
- **Make a set of mystery parcels.** Design and make wrappings for parcels so that they are easily distinguishable. Fill boxes with different materials making perhaps the largest also the lightest in weight.

    Draw a grid/chart as shown and a set of labels to show relationships.

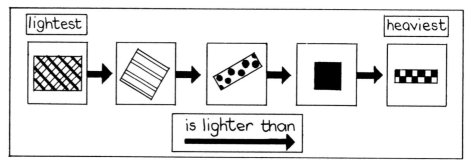

Start with two parcels and gradually increase to 3, 4, 5.

- **Individual worksheet.** Draw and label. Make a class book.

lighter than me	this is me	heavier than me

- Give each child a piece of clay or plasticine to make a model person or animal.
    - i) Compare the weight of one model with another, using a pan balance. Which is heavier?
    - ii) In a small group of children, arrange the models in order of weight.

Weigh out 10g of:
feathers
cubes
straw
sequins
sand
polystyrene

Hang your bag on the line.

Are you surprised?

- Set up a display table labelled "IT'S NOT WHAT YOU THINK!"
  Children compare the weights of similar objects, using a simple pan balance.

A DRY SPONGE	?	A WET SPONGE
A PUMICE STONE	?	A LARGE PEBBLE
A BALLOON	?	A BALLOON WITH AN OBJECT INSIDE
A SMALL BAG OF POLYSTYRENE	?	A SMALL BAG OF SAND
A PIECE OF BALSA WOOD	?	A PIECE OF PINE OF SIMILAR SIZE
A PLASTIC COTTON REEL	?	A WOODEN COTTON REEL
A PIECE OF ALUMINIUM OR SAUCEPAN/FRYING PAN	?	A PIECE OF IRON OR A CAST-IRON POT/FRYING PAN

- Investigate ways of making simple see-saw balances using junk materials, rulers and things available in the classroom.

Balances

- Give each child the same amount of clay or plasticine to make a model. Compare weights of finished models, and display.
- **Ask child to halve a ball of plasticine using a pan balance.** Roll half into a ball, and make a model with the other half. Display ball and model together on a grid.

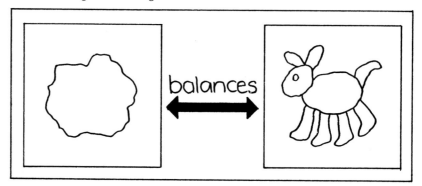

Using non-standard measures

- **Find things heavier than and lighter than one object.** Put into sets, label and draw.

- **Balance one object against sets of different objects.**

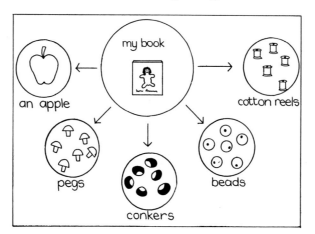

Individual worksheet or board large enough to put objects into circles.

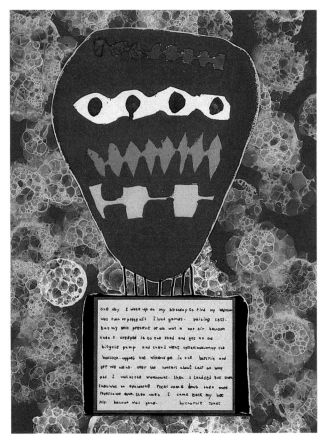

Display of written work and artwork (see Language Section, page 50)

- **Make a graph to record the comparison of different objects with the same non-standard units:**
    i) round or square beads, or cotton reels (strung), OR
    ii) conkers, bottle-tops, corks (glued).

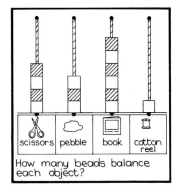

- **Compare equal numbers of different objects on a pan balance.**
    Draw what you see.

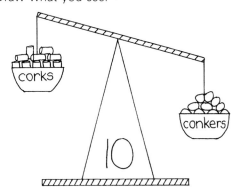

49

Introducing standard measures

- Feel how heavy a kg weight is! Make a display table with 1 kg amounts of sand, plasticine, bricks, stones, beads, flour, sugar, fruit.
- Make and draw a set of things heavier than 1 kg
  Make and draw a set of things lighter than 1 kg
- Peg out a washing line of bags containing 10 g of materials (see photo on page 47).
- Weigh your class pet at regular intervals (start with baby animal and chart the rate of increase).
- Weigh produce from the school garden. Find the total weight of the crop. Find the heaviest fruit or vegetable.

Cooking: • **Illustrate recipes**

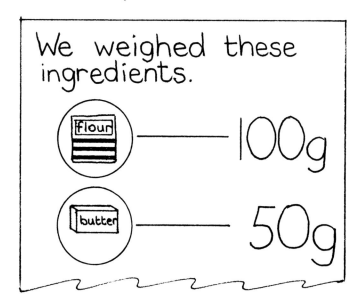

- Compare weight of biscuits and cakes before and after cooking. Observe colour, texture and taste, as well as weight.
- Make sweets to sell. Weigh out amounts 50 g and 100 g and package them attractively (e.g. coconut barfi, or coconut ice).

Science Activities:
- Investigate the effect of putting weights on a pendulum.
- Make model bridges with card and junk boxes. Which bridge supports the heaviest weight?
- Make weighted toys, balancing toys, and mobiles.

Language:
- Collect vocabulary: 'featherweight', 'lighter than air', 'light as a fairy', weightless, floating, leaden, 'tip the scales', 'sink like a stone', 'like a lead balloon'.
- Write imaginative stories: dreams of flying, floating, being weightless in space. Display stories on the baskets of painted balloons. Print the backing paper with blue and white bubble prints (See photo on page 49).
- Display 'heavy' stories on elephant shapes.
- Interview the school nurse about weighing children. Why is it necessary?

P.E., Music and Movement
- Lifting, pushing, pulling.
- Moving in a heavy or light way.
- Taking weight on different parts of the body.
- Moon-hopping, floating and jumping.

Research: Use *The Guinness Book of Records* to discover weight facts.

MONEY

Discussion: Why do we need money? What is pocket money? What are precious things? What is meant by "earning" money? Saving/spending? Money in history and in other cultures.

Collections: Commercially produced bags, till receipts, purses and wallets, foreign money, old cheque books/paying-in books, items connected with the Post Office or bank accounts that the children may have; money boxes and piggy banks.

Setting up shop in the classroom

The shop area must be well organised with clear access in and out of the "serving area"; shelving to display goods; a table top for a counter, and room to queue. A drawer for money is useful, as is a plentiful supply of carrier bags and purses.

Once the type of shop has been decided upon, a class discussion usually results in interesting suggestions for names. These can be written out and voted for. The results of the vote can be recorded on a graph, and a sign and logo designed and displayed.

Products for the shop can be made by the children, or brought from home by them. A clear system for running the shop needs to be devised, and **relevant notices displayed**.

Only 2 servers
behind the counter

Sharful and Laura
are the shopkeepers today

It is helpful for both children and teacher if the teacher takes the role of shopkeeper for the first few turns, to assess and supervise the activity and provide a model.

"Real" shopping is vitally important for young children. This experience can be arranged by holding a Christmas market, a sale of used toys, books, or produce baked by the class. Help from parents is needed for these "markets" to be successful.

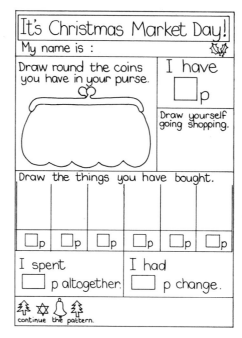

The money raised from a school shop could be used for a school requirement or outing (e.g. paying for a coach) or a charity.

The uses of the shop will progress from "play" to a "1p shop" to items priced in multiples of 5p and finally to items of any price.

Activities: Shop friezes:
Go and look at a row of shops, or photographs of shops. Ask questions to encourage observation. (If possible, include shops selling produce from other cultures.)

Where is the name of the shop? How is it written?

What is above the door? Where is the door?

Measure length of area allocated to the frieze, and divide by the number of children, to determine size of paper given to each child. Draw a stripe across the middle of the paper for the name of the shop. Discussion with the children will produce unusual and amusing shop names.

Posters:

What is the purpose of posters? How are they made to be noticed? The children will need to practise double lettering. Give them a clear task, e.g. "1p off everything!" and details to be included on the poster.

Carrier bags

Study examples of commercially produced paper carrier bags. Pull one apart. Allow each child one sheet of strong paper, glue and scissors.

Give instructions, e.g. "Make a bag to hold three items from the shop."

When made, the bags can be decorated with the names of the shops that the children painted for the frieze.

The bags can be displayed by pinning them to the wall, or from hooks on the shop, or in the form of a carrier bag "totem pole".

Money spiders

An amount of money is written on a black circle and the children draw eight legs, and glue coins on the legs, each totalling the amount on the body of the spider. (See photo of shop.)

How can I pay?
The children draw an item from the shop, and using arrows show different ways of making up the cost of the item (See photo of shop).
A hundred square
Using a large hundred square, show the 2, 5 and 10 families.

Precious or not?
Discuss what "precious" means. Does something have to be valuable to be precious? Ask the children to draw, colour and cut out something they think of as precious. Sort into two sets.

Suggestions for a stationery shop
Packets of crayons, felt-tip pens and pencils
Rubbers
Notebooks: paper stapled together with covers designed by the children
Pencil tops: made from clay or playdough
Clipboards: pieces of card (decorated) and bulldog clips
Wrapping paper made by the children
Envelopes
Greeting cards designed and written in by the children

Suggestions for a baker's shop
Fresh bread varnished with diluted P.V.A. glue.
Playdough cakes – tarts, Swiss rolls, sausage rolls, gateaux, buns.
Egg-carton cherry cakes in paper cases.

Suggestions for a greengrocer's shop
A greengrocer's shop gives an opportunity for the children to incorporate weighing in the shop. Root vegetables and hard fruit can be used fresh, but the children can also make produce.

Suggestions for a Toyshop

Felt finger puppets
Creatures made from socks
Yogurt pot people
Pom-pom animals
Bookmarks
Windmills
Clay/Playdough animals
Jewellery made from painted pasta shapes

Picture frames
Cars and trains made from matchboxes
Paper dolls with sets of clothes
Dolls made from rolled-up newspaper
Dolls' house furniture
Play theatres made from junk boxes
Jigsaws made from cutting up pictures
Teddies made with butterfly-clipped joints

Setting up a bank in the classroom

The children will begin to understand the notion of earning and saving money if a classroom bank is used in conjunction with their shop. It provides learning experiences across the curriculum.

Two counters are needed: one for transactions, with a coin drawer, and the other for storage of pens, pencils, stamp and ink pad, cheque books and paying-in books, scissors and calculators.

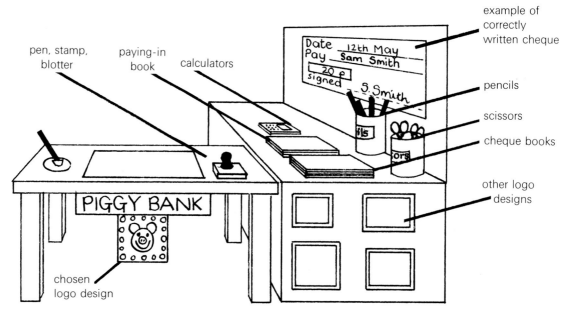

pen, stamp, blotter

paying-in book

calculators

example of correctly written cheque

Date _12th May_
Pay _Sam Smith_
_20 p_
signed _S.Smith_

pencils

scissors

cheque books

other logo designs

PIGGY BANK

chosen logo design

The process of banking needs very clear explanation, preferably in groups; the role of the cashier, the method of writing cheques and cheque stubs, and how to "sign" their names.

Having made items for the shop, the children can be 'paid' for their work by the teacher. The money is then used to open a bank account, and the amount is entered into the paying-in book. Before visiting the shop, the child withdraws money from the bank by writing a cheque.

The cheque book and paying-in books can be made with a duplicating master: three pages to one A4 sheet. Cut up, staple together, and cover with wallpaper to help the children recognise their own books in a pile.

Paying-in books

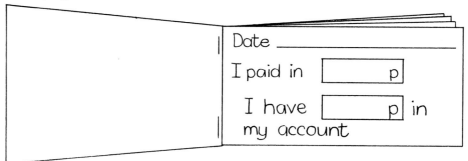

Date _____

I paid in [p]

I have [p] in my account

The initial entry is simple, but subsequent entries should take into account how much the child has saved in his/her account already.

Cheque books

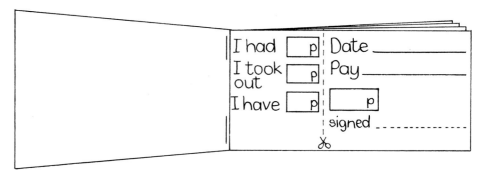

I had [p] Date _____
I took out [p] Pay _____
I have [p] [p]
signed -------------

The stub is used to keep an account of their savings.

Plaster-cast coins

Study and sort coins: heads and tails, colour, value, date of manufacture, country of origin.

Using a circular piece of paper, let the children design a coin, either head or tail, including the writing.

Roll out soft plasticine, cut to fit the base of a shallow circular margarine tub, and draw the design onto the plasticine. (N.B. Writing must be in reverse, so hold paper up to a window and copy from the reverse side.)

Put the plasticine in the tub. Mix the plaster of Paris and pour in to a depth of 1" ($2\frac{1}{2}$–3 cm.) (N.B. Add plaster to cold water, stirring continuously until all powder is in the solution and has a creamy consistency). Knock the base of the tub to let air out. Leave to set.

(Point out the change from liquid to solid, and the heat which is given off).

Turn out, and paint with gold, silver or bronze paint, and varnish with diluted P.V.A. glue.

(N.B. Never throw liquid plaster down the drain. Allow it to dry and throw away any left over).

If you want to hang the coins, stick a pencil upright into the plasticine before the plaster is poured in. When dry, remove the pencil and thread a ribbon through the hole.

Display on a dark, rich-coloured cloth, preferably velvet.
Vary the levels of the surface by using screwed up newspaper underneath.

Purses

● **Binca:** Start with a rectangle. The children could plan their designs first on paper, taking into account where the folds will be. Sew the sides. Fasten with a press-stud and make a handle with French knitting.

Drawstring: Fold a rectangle in half and sew up the sides. Hem the top. Using a material hole-puncher, make a line of holes and thread the drawstring through them. A design could be embroidered on the purse.

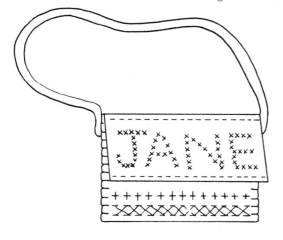

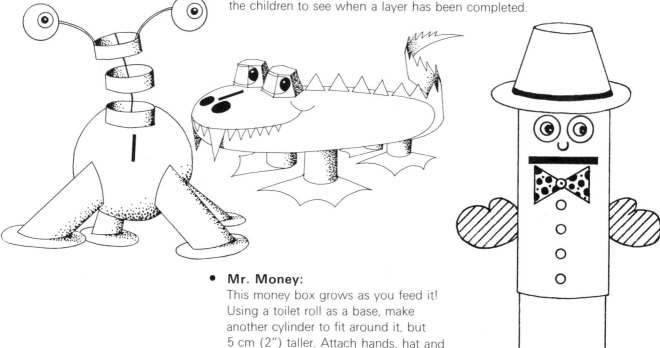

- **Piggybanks:**
  Use a pâpier maché covered balloon to create weird and wonderful creatures. N.B. Always use a glue without fungicide. Two colours of newspaper help the children to see when a layer has been completed.

- **Mr. Money:**
  This money box grows as you feed it! Using a toilet roll as a base, make another cylinder to fit around it, but 5 cm (2") taller. Attach hands, hat and face to the outer roll, and feet to the toilet roll. Cut a mouth no more than 5 cm (2") from the top.

- Bank Note designs:
  Study bank notes from many countries to find out the information on them. Why is the design so complex? Look for the watermarks and silver strips. (Older children could use rulers and compasses for their designs.)

- **Coin Rubbings:**

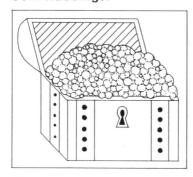

i) Make sure that the rubbing medium is soft and that paper is thin, or
ii) Put coins under a sheet of silver foil, and press or rub to produce subtle relief images which can be used to "fill" a treasure chest with silver coins.

Language:
- "If I were a millionaire. . . ."
- "My most precious thing"
- Shopping lists
- Finding buried treasure
- Invitations to a class "market"

Drama:
- Everyday situations in the shop. Provide dressing-up clothes, hats etc.
- Shopping: getting lost in a crowd
  saving up and spending
  spoilt for choice!
  a busy marketplace

Music: Using percussion and voice, create the sounds of a market.

Birthdays

The weekly birthday assembly

The birthday assembly

- Birthday calendar, see page 62.
- Make a pretend birthday cake (cardboard around tin). Light correct number of candles. Sing song "One birthday candle when you're one year old".
- Make a 3-D graph. Each 'birthday child' makes a tower of bricks to represent his/her number of years.
- Draw "rainbow" numerals (see page 10), with each child contributing a colour on the appropriate numeral.
- **Make birthday cards and badges** to present to the children.
- Set up the birthday calendar display as shown in the photograph. Make two sets of names-of-months cards. Display one set as a frieze. Use the other set to show the date and the day of the week on a Breakthrough, or similar, wordstand.

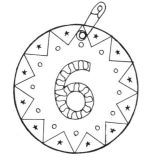

Friday 12th June 1988

- Collect birthday stories and poems to read.

Birthdays
Further birthday activities

- **Sort children into sets** according to their age. Move them from set to set as they have a birthday.

We are 5 years old.   We are 6 years old.   We are 7 years old.

January   February   March

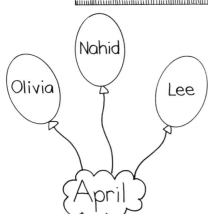

- **Birthday months graphs:**
  i) Children draw themselves holding the correct number of balloons.
  ii) Each child makes a cake shape, decorated with doilies, tissue and foil. Number of candles (drinking straws) show the age of each child.
  iii) Children draw self-portraits and put them into a large balloon-shaped set which is matched to the birthday month.
  iv) Match individually named balloon shapes to months.

- Design and make birthday cards (incorporate age of child).
- Design and make birthday invitations.
- Design and make party hats.
- Design and make fancy dress for a theme party.
- Paint birthday party pictures and collages. **Make pretend party foods and display on plates.**

- Make a birthday calendar for your family. Include festivals and anniversaries and family celebrations.
- Research: birthday celebrations in other cultures.
- Calculate with a calculator. How many months old are you? How many weeks old are you? How many days old are you? (Birthday children will find this easier).

Calendars

- Compile a whole school calendar by collecting pieces of artwork together with children's writings. (See photo above)

- **Sliding Calendar:**
  List the names of the months on an oblong piece of card. Make a circular face with a hat and hands attached. Cut two slits for the mouth and slot the oblong through so that each month can be seen in turn. Glue feet to the bottom of the oblong and add a calendar pad to the bottom or to the hat, if wanted.

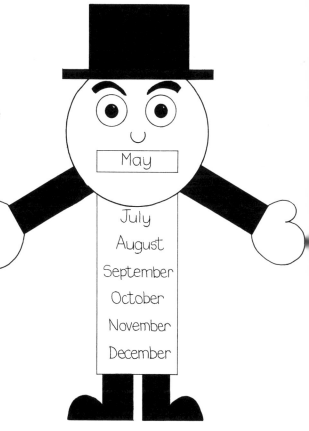

- **Four Seasons Calendar:**
  Make outlines by 'blowing' inks with a straw, and use felt-tip pens to complete the pictures.

  Add seasonal details with collage pieces.

  Four colours of backing paper:
  Winter – white
  Summer – blue
  Spring – yellow
  Autumn – pale orange

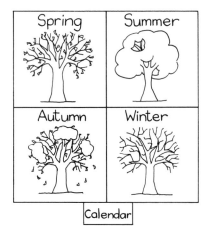

Calendars

- **Circular calendar**
  Spring, Summer, Autumn and Winter pictures in each quarter.

  Fix circle with butterfly clip.

Calendar

- **Solid shape with twelve faces.** Glue page from calendar on each face.

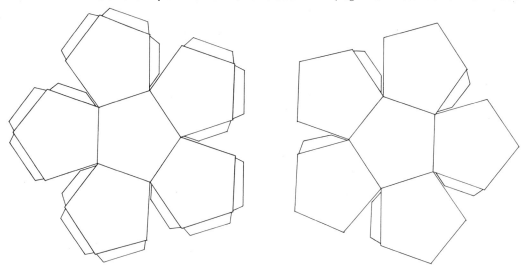

- **Birthday calendar**
  Make large calendar grid for each month. Use the chart for counting on and back: finding today's date, tomorrow's, yesterday's. Mark school holidays and special festivals on the chart. The birthday children draw a picture of themselves on a prepared piece of paper. This is matched to the chart with a streamer or ribbon. (See photo p. 59.)

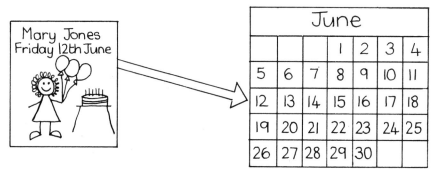

Mary Jones
Friday 12th June

June						
			1	2	3	4
5	6	7	8	9	10	11
12	13	14	15	16	17	18
19	20	21	22	23	24	25
26	27	28	29	30		

The set of twelve month charts can be made into a book at the end of the year. (Pictures could be glued on facing pages).

Days of the week

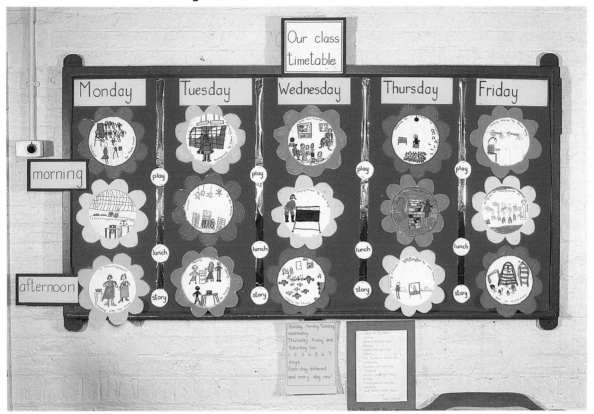

- Make a class timetable showing the activities for each day of the week. Children draw on each circle – illustrating the week's activities, e.g. cooking, sewing, gym, maths.
- **Display timetable on trains.** Put helpers/parents in the carriages.

- Older children can design their own timetables and devise flow diagrams.
- **Fold paper into three sections.** Children can write a sentence about activities using future, present and past. Make into a class book.

yesterday	today	tomorrow
I went swimming	I am writing in school	I shall go to my friend's house

Days of the week

- **Write "days of the week" poems.** Use "Ways of the Week" by John Kitching (see book reference) as a stimulus. Hang as a mobile or mount on wall.

- **Make up "days of the week" stories** ("On Friday something funny happened ..." "On Monday ...", "On Tuesday. ...").

Sam's Week	Monday	Tuesday	Wednesday
	1.	2.	3.
Thursday	**Friday**	**Saturday**	**Sunday**
4.	5.	6.	7.

- Keep individual diaries over a period of time, e.g. two weeks. Decorate covers and illustrate.
- **'Weather chart'** recording weather conditions over a period of time. Illustrate each day, and make a wall strip for the whole month.

Sunday 1st May	Monday 2nd May	Tuesday 3rd May	Wednesday 4th May	Thursday 5th May	Friday 6th May	Saturday 7th May

Analyse data – how many days with rain?
– how many days without?

- Where can you find dates? Collect packages with date stamps, on letters and envelopes, newspapers and magazines, tickets, cheques, appointment cards, birth certificates and passports. Why do we need to put dates on things?
- Investigate the names of the days of the week. Research origins.
- **Display date** (day, month and year) on Breakthrough, or similar, stand, using prepared cards as in birthday display.

Night and day

Discussion: Talk about sunrise, sunset; opposites; light and dark; people who work at night; nocturnal animals; story or poetry stimulus.

Collections: Pictures of night scenes and busy day scenes; sunrise and sunset pictures; pictures of shadows.

Art and Craft Activities:

- Paint to show the contrast of dark with light. (Black and white patterns or light and dark shades of the same colour.)

- **Record important activities of the day around a circle:** word cards make the rays around the sun.

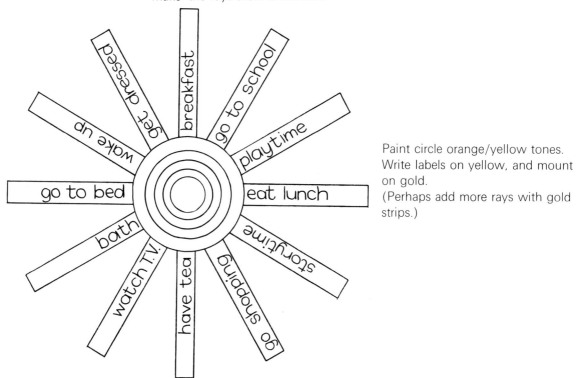

Paint circle orange/yellow tones. Write labels on yellow, and mount on gold.
(Perhaps add more rays with gold strips.)

- Paint sunrise/sunset pictures using the wet paper technique. Make silhouette shapes by blow-painting with black ink, or by tearing and cutting from black paper. (See photo p. 25.)

- Make a day and night zig-zag book.

Night and day

- Shadows:
  i) Collect photographs of shadows. Take photographs in school playground.
  ii) Measure your shadow at different times of the day.
  iii) Make shadow puppets on sticks.
  iv) Make shadow shapes with your hand, draw around the shapes and paint. Make 'creatures' out of your hand silhouette.

- **Day and Night mobiles:**

  Cover hoop with black crêpe, and use black or silver thread for hanging.

  Sun – gold, orange and yellow collage. Cover hoop with blue crêpe. Use blue thread.

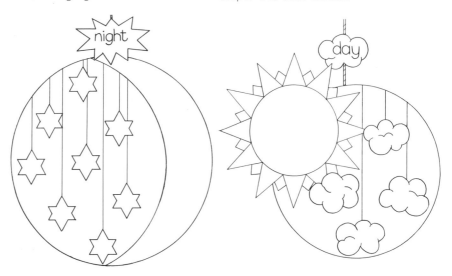

Night and Day pictures and writing can be mounted on the stars or cloud shapes. (Use moon hoop for hanging 'cone witches' at Hallowe'en.)

- **Day and Night display board:**

  DAY: Backing paper blue
  Sunburst streamers – yellow crêpe or gold strips
  Display writing or paintings mounted on gold
  Sun – painted in shades of yellow and orange

  NIGHT: Backing paper purple or black tissue
  Sponge silver stars using stencil or by masking
  Display writing or paintings mounted on silver
  Moon – milk bottle tops, sequins, silver foil

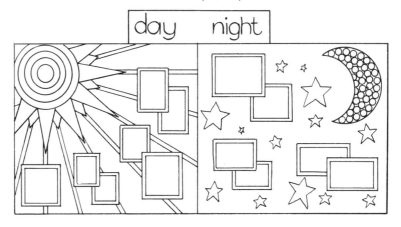

Clocks

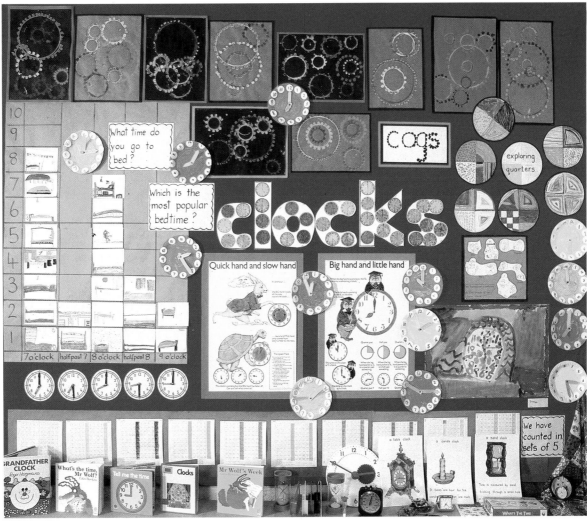

Discussion: What do clocks do? Why do we need to measure time? What is your favourite time of day? How many clocks do you have in your house? Which machines have timers? When does time seem to pass slowly, or quickly?

Collections: Different kinds of clocks, old and new; watches, timers, e.g. egg-timers, sand timers, cooking timers, metronomes; 'tockers', cardboard clocks, geared clocks, broken clocks, cog-wheels, springs and dials; pictures of clocks.

Maths activities: • **Make an illustrated time line** with hours of the day marked.

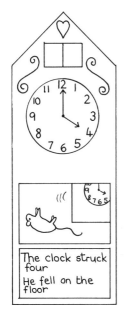

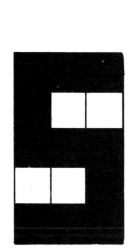

The clock struck four
He fell on the floor

- Make an illustrated time line for the whole school showing important times of the day. Set cardboard clocks to show correct times.
- **Make a wall-story or class (zig-zag) book.** Extend the rhyme "Hickory Dickory Dock", e.g. "The clock struck three, The mouse climbed a tree."
  Make the pages of the book or panels of the wall-story clock-shaped; each page to have a clear clockface, the verse of the rhyme and an illustration.
  (It is difficult to rhyme with 'twelve' – use 'noon' or 'mid-night' instead)
- 'Time' storybooks: Use *The Bad-tempered Ladybird* (see book reference p. 70) or "What's the time, Mr. Wolf?" (see book reference p. 70) as a stimulus, e.g.   "at 1 o'clock the elephant....."
                             "at 2 o'clock the elephant ....." etc.
  Illustrate each page with picture and clockface showing the time.
- Make cardboard clocks on painted paper plates (use stickers for numbers).
- Explore halves and quarters of a circle. Colour the segments.

Timing activities:
- **Make a large chart "What can you do in one minute?"**

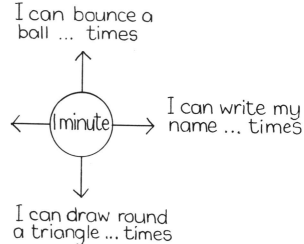

I can bounce a ball ... times

I can put ... pegs in a board ← 1 minute → I can write my name ... times

I can draw round a triangle ... times

- Children time their journeys to school, lunch sittings, walk around the school.
- Plan activities to last a set time, e.g. make a 30 minute tape to send to a penfriend, or a tape for a classmate in hospital.

Art and Craft:
- **Draw digital numbers on squared paper.** Given height and width of numbers, how many squares are needed for each number? How many lines did you need to draw for each? Use a 3×5 frame.
- **Make cog pictures.** Print circles with tubes, saucers. Paint or print cogs (end of coloured rods, Lego brick – see photo on previous page).
- Look at the inside of old clocks. Make close observational drawings of the cogs, springs and 'workings'.
- Design clocks for different rooms in the house. Design clocks for different buildings, e.g. a police station, a fire station, a hospital, a school, a baker's shop, greengrocer's shop.

Language:
- Illustrate stories such as "The Hare and the Tortoise".
- Collect, investigate and illustrate sayings, e.g. 'how time flies', 'the early bird catches the worm', 'till the cows come home', 'quick as lightning' and 'in the twinkling of an eye'.

CALENDAR OF FESTIVALS

Display to celebrate the Chinese New Year

SPRING (March, April, May)

Holi	Feb.–March	Hindu
Mothering Sunday	March	Christian
Easter	March–April	Christian
Passover	April	Jewish
Baisakhi Day	April	Sikh
Shavuot (Pentecost)	May	Jewish
Vesak	May	Buddhist
Whitsuntide	May	Christian

SUMMER (June, July, August)

Raksha Bandha	July/August	Hindu
Janam Ashtami	August	Hindu

AUTUMN (September, October, November)

Rosh Hashanah and Yom Kippur	Sept./Oct.	Jewish
Harvest Festival	Sept./Oct.	Christian
Succoth	Sept./Oct.	Jewish
Divali	October	Hindu
Hallowe'en	31st October	
Guy Fawkes Night	5th November	
St. Nicholas' Day	6th December	Christian

WINTER (December, January, February)

Birthday of Guru Nanak	November	Sikh
Hanukah	December	Jewish
Advent	27th Nov.– 25th Dec.	Christian
Christmas	25th Dec.	Christian
New Year	1st January	
Chinese New Year	Jan./Feb.	
Valentine's Day	14th Feb.	
Purim	Feb./March	Jewish
Lent	Feb./March	Christian

FESTIVALS WHICH MOVE THROUGH THE SEASONS

Ramadan	Islamic
Id-ul-Fitr	Islamic
Meelad-al-Nabil	Islamic

BOOK REFERENCES

Maths resource books for teachers

Childsplay Mathematics, Lyndon Baker, Peter Wells, Jo Stephens, David Fielker, pub. by Evans Bros.
Pointers, School Mathematics Project, pub. by Cambridge University Press.
Points of Departure 1 and 2, Tansy Hardy, Anne Haworth, Eric Love, Alistair McIntosh, pub. by Association of Teachers of Mathematics.
Mathematical Activities from Poland, Jerzy Cwirko-Godycki, pub. by Association of Teachers of Mathematics.
Mathskill, 1 and 2, By Roger Hepworth, pub. by Piccolo.
The Puffin Number and Shape Book, Rose Griffiths, pub. by Puffin.
A Way with Maths, by Nigel Langdon and Charles Snape, Cambridge University Press.
Teaching Mathematics 7–13, by Edith Biggs, pub. by NFER, Nelson.
The Guinness Mathematics Book, by Leonard Marsh, pub. by GBR Educational Ltd.
Mathematical Activities, by Brian Bolt, pub. by Cambridge University Press.
Primary Mathematics Today, by Elizabeth Williams and Hilary Shuard, pub. by Longman.
Nuffield Maths, 1 and 2, Teachers' Handbooks, by Monica Williams and Winifred Moore, pub. by Longman.
Teaching Mathematics, 5–9, by Edith Biggs and Joan Sutton, pub. by McGraw-Hill.
Let's Celebrate, Maurice Lynch, pub. by Ginn & Co.
Festive Occasions, Judy Ridgway, pub. by Oxford University Press.

Number: **Stories:**
1 Hunter, by Pat Hutchins, Picture Puffins.
Teddybears, 1–10, Susanna Gretz, Picture Lions.
Ten, nine, eight, Molly Bang, Picture Puffins.
Ten Sleepy Sheep, Holly Keller, Hippo.
Counting on an Elephant, Jill MacDonald, Picture Puffins.
The Bad Babies Counting Book, Tony Bradman, Beaver Books.
The doorbell rang, Pat Hutchins, Picture Puffins.
The Shopping Basket, John Burningham, Picture Lions.
Sixes and Sevens, John Yeoman and Quentin Blake, Picture Mac.
1, 2, 3 to the zoo, Eric Carle, Hamish Hamilton.

Poems:
'Porwigles', Julie Holder, in *A First Poetry Book*, Oxford University Press.
'Six Little Mice', Trad., in *Roger was a Razor Fish*, Bodley Head.
'Making Tens', M. M. Hutchinson, in *The Book of a Thousand Poems*, Evans Bros.
'Ten Little Dicky Birds', A. W. I. Baldwin, in *The Book of a Thousand Poems*.
'Count Down', Colin Ramsay, in *Word Spinning*, Evans Bros.

Songs:
'This Old Man', Trad.
'One More River', Trad.
'One Man Came to Mow', Trad.
'When I was One', in *The Funny Family*, collected by Alison McMorland, Ward Lock Educ.
'Ten in the bed', Trad.
'Dumplins', in *Mango Spice*, A. & C. Black.
'Dice Song', in *Game-Songs with Prof. Dogg's Troupe*, A. & C. Black.
Spring: 'Spring has Sprung', in *Harlequin*, A. & C. Black.
Christmas: 'Twelve Days of Christmas', in *Mango Spice*, A. & C. Black.
Machines: 'Machines', in *Kokoleoko*, Macmillan Education Ltd.
Autumn: 'Paintbox', in *Harlequin*, A. & C. Black.
Space: '5 Little Men in a Flying Saucer', in *The Music Box Songbook*, BBC Books.
Fireworks: '5th of November', *Harlequin*, A. & C. Black.
Minibeasts: 'Caterpillars only crawl', *Harlequin*, A. & C. Black.

Measuring: **Stories:**
Jim and the Beanstalk, Raymond Briggs, Picture Puffin.
The BFG, Roald Dahl, Puffin.
The Iron Man, Ted Hughes, Faber and Faber.
The Dinosaur's Footprint, Richard Blythe, Macdonald Starters.
Flat Stanley, Jeff Brown, Magnet.
Lengthy, Syd Hoff, World's Work.
Mrs. Pepperpot, Alf Prøyser, Young Puffin.
The Shrinking of Treehorn, F. P. H. Heide, Young Puffin.
The Bad Babies Counting Book, Tony Bradman, Beaver Books.
Peepo! Janet and Allan Ahlberg, Picture Puffin.